EXPLAINING
Studying the Bible

DAVID PAWSON

ANCHOR RECORDINGS

Copyright © 2016 David Pawson

The right of David Pawson to be identified as author of this Work has been asserted by him in accordance with the Copyright, Designs and Patents Act 1988.

First published in Great Britain in 2016 by
Anchor Recordings Ltd
Synegis House, 21 Crockhamwell Road,
Woodley, Reading RG5 3LE

No part of this publication may be reproduced or transmitted in any form or by any means, electronic or mechanical, including photocopy, recording or any information storage and retrieval system, without prior permission in writing from the publisher.

For more of David Pawson's teaching,
including DVDs and CDs, go to
www.davidpawson.com

FOR FREE DOWNLOADS
www.davidpawson.org

For further information,
email: info@davidpawsonministry.com

ISBN 978-1-911173-31-1

Printed by Lightning Source

This booklet is based on a talk. Originating as it does from the spoken word, its style will be found by many readers to be somewhat different from my usual written style. It is hoped that this will not detract from the substance of the biblical teaching found here.

As always, I ask the reader to compare everything I say or write with what is written in the Bible and, if at any point a conflict is found, always to rely upon the clear teaching of scripture.

David Pawson

EXPLAINING
Studying the Bible

I would like to begin by asking you five questions that you can answer to yourself. Firstly, do you believe that the Bible is the Word of God? Then, do you believe that it is the most important book anyone could ever read? Next, have you read it – not bits of it, all of it? Now, have you read any other book through? Now, in answering this last question, think carefully about it, because God will be a witness to your answer. Last question, are you going to read it – all of it?

Read three chapters a day and five on Sunday and you will be through it in twelve months, so there is a little target for you. I admit it is a very difficult book to read when you first get hold of it. I think the first thing that puts you off is the size of it. There are 750,000 words. You rarely read a book so big. It is a lot of words in one book.

I have something that was given to me when I was six years old and was then the smallest Bible in the world, so small that it fits into a matchbox. It is leather-bound and even has pictures in it, and when I was six I could read it with my own eyes. I can't now, but there is a little magnifying glass in the front cover which helps you to read it. I also now have the present "smallest Bible in the world", a little piece of micro-film, a tiny piece of plastic the size of a large postage stamp, and every word of the Bible is on that – each dot is a whole chapter and I have read it with an ordinary microscope of 200x magnification and it is a very handy way of carrying the whole Bible around in your pocket. The only disadvantage is that you need to carry a microscope as well!

But in reality, it is a large book and it takes a lot of time to work through it. But that is not the biggest problem, even though it is 1500 pages, with the print like a newspaper in two columns – not very attractive to read. They have tried producing Bibles with pictures for those who just like looking at pictures, but that doesn't help much. The biggest problem in studying the Bible is the cultural gap between you and the Bible. It was written at least two thousand years ago and many miles away from here in a totally different culture, and that creates a problem. We are reading a Bible that is quite different from our daily newspaper. After all, have you ever felt bursting with curiosity to know what happened to the Amorites? Has that ever been on your horizon? We are just not in touch, it is a different world. There were no telecommunications, nothing such as we have now – no television, no cars, nothing – a different world. It is a different culture. How are we going to read it?

And when you get to the genealogies, the first nine chapters of the first book of Chronicles are names, and apparently all they did for hundreds of years was "begat" – So and So begat So and So, etc. It is like reading the telephone directory, and who enjoys reading that? When we read the Bible right through in our church, it took eighty-two and a half hours. We were quicker than some as the average reading aloud takes eighty-four hours. We began Sunday night and finished Thursday breakfast time. Somebody had to read all those names in Chronicles and it was a tedious business, and that is not the only genealogy in the Bible.

The Bible is a History Book
So I understand people who find it hard to read and study the Bible. What kind of a book is it? Well, at first glance when you open it, it is a history book. But it is a unique history book as it is different from every other history book that you will find in a public library. The difference is this: it begins earlier and ends later than any other history book in the world. It begins right at the beginning of our universe, and ends with the end of our universe and the beginning of another one. No other history book is as comprehensive as that. So, do we read it just as a history book? No. Unfortunately, the books are not in the right chronological order and whoever arranged the prophets decided to put the biggest first and the smallest last, disregarding altogether when they were written. So we have Isaiah, Jeremiah and Ezekiel first and then it goes all the way through the small ones to the end.

The same kind of arrangement applies to Paul's letters. What is the longest one he wrote? Romans. What is the smallest one he wrote? Philemon. So they put Romans first and Philemon last and they are totally in the wrong order. Actually, some people do read the Bible purely as history. I am very impressed with the writing of a scholar called David Rohl. He is not a believer but he is now totally convinced of the historical accuracy of the Old Testament from his research into archaeology, and he said it is the most reliable book from that age historically. He is very impressed, and has even located the Garden of Eden for us by studying all the hints in Genesis chapter 2. And when he found the lovely valley surrounded by hills he found it was still full of fruit trees. Isn't that interesting? Maybe you have eaten fruit from that valley without knowing it. But some people – including David Rohl – read the Bible purely as history.

The Bible is a Book of Romance

You could also say that the Bible is a book of romance – a very romantic book. In fact, if you open the Bible dead centre it opens at an erotic love song called Song of Solomon which never mentions God, prayer, salvation or anything spiritual at all – yet it is in the Bible. But the whole Bible is a romantic story and in fact it is the story of a Father looking for a Bride for his Son. That is romantic enough, and like every good romance it finishes with the wedding. I always think it is a funny habit that romantic novels finish up by saying: "... and they got married and lived happily ever after." You know there was one misprint in a romantic novel – the last sentence read: "... and they got married and lived happily even after", which I thought was perhaps nearer the truth. Nevertheless our Bible ends with the wedding. Jesus called himself the Bridegroom and the church is called the Bride and it is one big romance from beginning to end.

A Library of Books

But actually there are parts of it that don't fit into that category either. The truth is that the Bible is not a book, it is a library of sixty-six books, and that is one of the most important things I can say. It is not *a* book – the very name "Bible" was originally plural (*Biblia*), which means "books". It is a library of separate books, each one of them different from the other sixty-five, and it is only when you find out the character of each book that you begin to understand the Bible better. I am advocating that you read the Bible a book at a time, that you don't dip into it here and there and read a little here and a little there – that is not how you would treat any other book – rather, treat each book as a book. God gave us his Word in books and therefore that is how he wanted us to read it. To read it a book at a time changes your whole understanding of the Bible. That is why I wrote the book *Unlocking the Bible* – to help people read it a book at a time. I will tell you the story of how I wrote it.

I was approached by the pastors of a little town in the Thames Valley in England, and they said, "David, our people are not studying the Bible for themselves. They'll come and listen to preachers; they'll sing – they love singing and music – but they're not reading the Bible at home for themselves. Can you do anything about it?" I agreed to try and said I would go one Sunday evening a month for four months. Each of those four evenings I would spend telling them about one book in the Bible, and my aim would be to get them so interested in that book that they couldn't wait to get home and read it. But I would go only on the condition that they would all read the book before I came, that they would read it again after I had been, that all the preachers in the churches would preach from that book for the next month, and all the house groups would study that book for the next month so that at the end of one month they could say they felt they knew one book.

My aim was not only to get them so interested in the book that they couldn't wait to read it but to give them enough information – background material and insight into the book – so that when they read it they got excited with that book.

So I went for the first evening, and three more, and I said "Now you know four books." And the pastors all came to me again and said, "David, please can we book you for six years." I told them I might be in heaven by then. But actually we did it, and once a month for six years I went to that little group of churches and took them through one book in the Bible. Well, I used photographs, maps, charts, models – anything that would get them excited about the book – and it was recorded, but only in audio, and those recordings went out everywhere so quickly. But immediately I began to get complaints that people could not see the photos, maps, models or charts mentioned in the talks. So somebody came to me and said I would have to do the whole lot again, but this time on video. "Oh," I said, "I can't face that!" But they persuaded me, and the next few years I spent going through the Bible again – book by book – and including on the videos the aids I had used. Then, after that was finished, I heaved a sigh of relief and thought, "That's that!"

Then a top publisher in London came and said, "David, it's all got to be written down in a book" – and I said, "Oh No! I can't face all that again!" So they did get hold of a young man who transcribed the sound track of the videos and then he put it into some form of shape and I edited it and just polished it up – and that was how *Unlocking the Bible* was written. So it took about twelve to fifteen years to write. But that was the fruit of just a few pastors coming and asking me to come and help their people to read the Bible. It is history to me now.

How to Study the Bible

Now, how to study the Bible? Well, let me begin by saying how not to. There are a number of ways people read the Bible. One is what I call the "Lucky Dip". Do you know what I mean by that? It is amazing how many use that method – like a man who randomly pointed his finger at a verse and read: "Judas went out and hanged himself." So he quickly changed his place and pointed again, only to read: "Go and do thou likewise." That is no way to read the Bible.

Some people treat it like a dose of medicine – "Twelve verses a day keep the Devil away." So they duly read their little bit just to keep him away. Some treat their Bible reading like a horoscope – reading in the stars. They read it and hope that something in it will just fit their life for that day. Don't try to read the Bible like that. Sometimes it might work, but God didn't intend you to read the Bible like that, just picking a text out that fits your situation. A young businessman came to me and he said, "David, I'm thinking of buying a shop in the middle of Birmingham to turn it into a coffee bar for outreach to young people. I asked the Lord to give me guidance as to whether I should buy it, and I found a text in my daily reading that said 'I have much blessing in store for you' – do you think God has given me enough guidance to buy the store?" I said: "No, unless he gives you more guidance than that, don't spend your money." But people can find just a word that speaks to them like that. Sometimes God uses that, to my amazement. I wouldn't, but he sometimes does.

A friend of mine bought an aeroplane many years ago – £3,800 he paid for it, secondhand. He was reading his Bible and he found this in the book of Revelation: "I saw an angel flying in the midst of heaven to take the eternal gospel to the people of the world." He believed that was a word from God, so that aeroplane became the beginning – the first plane – of a missionary air force that is now operating worldwide, called the Missionary Aviation Fellowship. My first flight was in that plane. I have to admit that God used that word though it is about an angel, not about an aeroplane, but he took it as guidance and God has honoured that Air Force. That was just after World War Two and the first crew of that plane are still alive, and I am in touch with them even today. But it is not God's usual way of guidance, and if you try to find some word that would just fit your situation, you might and you might not.

Many people try to use Bible reading notes of some great preacher. Well, I am afraid if you use Bible reading notes, I won't guarantee it but I think you will read the notes more than the Bible. You will read the passage for the day and then you will study the notes. I want people to study the

Bible, not notes about the Bible. That is being spoon fed by someone else. I want to encourage people to get into it for themselves and discover its treasures for themselves. So my book *Unlocking the Bible* does not read the Bible for you – far from it – but it gets you into the Bible. I have had so many letters and phone calls saying, "I'm now enjoying reading my Bible." That is the best reward I could have.

So there are ways not to read the Bible and there are ways to read it. I am advocating that you treat the Bible as a library and read it a whole book at a time. What other book would you treat as you treat the Bible? If you got hold of one of Agatha Christie's books, would you start reading in chapter 13 and read a paragraph, then turn back to chapter 5 and read a bit there, then turn to the end of the book and read how it ends? Darting about a book like that, you will never get the message of the book. You need to read the book, and therefore before you begin to study any part of the Bible, read the book through and find out the answer to one question: why was this book written? Once you have that answer, that key will unlock the whole book to you and make it a different book. Until you have that answer, you can read bits of it and they simply will not make sense the way God meant them to. You might get some sense out of a verse or a few verses, but they've been placed in a book for a reason.

The Bible has been Divided

Let me now go back to what I call a "bee in my bonnet" – something that buzzes round my brain. The chapter numbers and verse numbers were never intended by God. There were no chapter and verse numbers in the books of the Bible for hundreds of years. You had to know your way round the Bible by context. You couldn't look up a text. So, in those early days, they "searched the scriptures". We don't do that now, we look them up, and I am not one of the preachers who say, "Now look up Hezekiah 3:16" (which doesn't actually exist, but you know what I mean). I once said that in a meeting and I saw someone get their Bible and flick through it – where's Hezekiah 3:16? I told them it said: "Thou shalt not go to the cinema on Sunday", and they were looking it up, trying to find it. But you know what I mean.

I don't say to look up this chapter so-and-so and this verse so-and-so. I only do what the apostles did – they said, "You'll find it in Isaiah", and you had to read the whole of Isaiah to find what they were saying, and that is good for you. By the way, did you know that God whistles? Did you know that? It's twice in the book of Isaiah, but I am not going to tell you the chapters and the verses because God didn't want his Word in chapters and verses. How did they get in there? Well, the chapters got in, I am sad to say, by an Archbishop of Canterbury. He was called Stephen Langton and I can even give you the year (1205), and he decided to divide God's Word up into chapters and he spent a long time doing so.

So that is why you have it in chapters, and some of those chapter divisions come in the worst possible place and split up what God meant to be together. I will give you four examples of that. In the book of Genesis, the six days of creation are in chapter one but the seventh day is in chapter two, and that belongs with the rest. He has put a chapter division in there which splits off the story of creation on the seventh day from the other six. Or let us take one of my favourite chapters and yours – Isaiah 53. It is a song about the Suffering Servant of God who is suffering for the sins of his people and it has those majestic verses: "He was wounded for our transgressions, he was bruised for our iniquities, the chastisement of our peace was upon him, and with his stripes we are healed." You know the chapter – it is a song. But the first verses of the song are at the end of chapter 52 which is rarely read in connection with chapter 53. The first verses of a song are vital to the song – they set the tone, the theme, and they introduce you to the song. But people read Isaiah 53 without reading the end of Isaiah 52.

Take two examples from the New Testament: one is in Acts 18 and 19. At the beginning of chapter 19, Paul comes to Ephesus and he finds some Christian disciples, but something is missing and so he asks them, "Did you receive the Holy Spirit when you believed?" And they said, "What is the Holy Spirit?" How could you have Christian disciples that didn't know the Holy Spirit? Well, you can. There are plenty today, but why were there Christian disciples in Ephesus who had not been told about the Holy Spirit? The answer is that the preacher they had had was a man called Apollos who was learned in all the scriptures – he knew the Bible, as much as they had in his day, and he knew Jesus and he talked about both of those – but he had never told them about the Holy Spirit because he didn't know the Holy Spirit himself. And all that is in chapter 18! So you will never understand chapter 19 if you don't read chapter 18 first.

The biggest, worst example of chapter divisions is in the book of Revelation. Revelation is full of sevens – there are seven churches and seven letters to those seven churches at the beginning, and each of the letters has seven parts. Later in the book of Revelation you read about seven seals and then seven trumpets and then seven bowls of wrath poured out on the earth. Everybody thinks that is the end of sevens and it isn't. The book ends with seven visions which belong together but are rarely read together because they are split over three chapters – chapters 19, 20 and 21. Because the seven visions are spread over those three chapters, people don't realise there are seven right at the end of the book of Revelation, and that split has had very serious consequences.

Have you ever heard of pre-millennial, post-millennial, a-millennial with regard to the return of the Lord? That controversy is due to the splitting of those seven visions into three chapters – and how Christians have argued! Some Christians now say, "I am pan-millennial and that means that everything will 'pan out alright in the end'." That is a "cop out". A friend of mine landed at Belfast airport, Northern Ireland, where you have a lot of people who want to put you in a category very quickly if you are a preacher. They said to my friend. "Are you a-millennial, pre-millennial or post-millennial, and my friend said, "That is a pre-post-erous question," which I thought was a very neat answer.

But all that argument came out of the chapter divisions in the last series of seven visions. So, try to forget the chapter numbers, and above all forget the verse numbers. The latter were added by a printer who lived in Paris, called Stephanus. He had to travel from Paris to Lyon and he travelled by coach and horses which made it a very long journey. Well, he had his Bible with him already divided into chapters, and to while away the time on the journey he divided the chapters into verses, and he did it for our convenience but it has damaged our understanding of the Bible.

The word "text" has changed its meaning totally as the result of those verse numbers. Originally, text – the text of the Bible – meant the whole Bible. In normal English it still means the whole of a book – the text of the book. But in Christian circles the "text" has come to mean one sentence in a book, one verse. And we started throwing texts at each other – so often out of context – and we have missed the real meaning of the text because we have taken it out.

I sometimes ask an audience or congregation if they know John 3:16. Many hands are raised. Then I ask how many could tell me John 3:17, and usually only a few hands are raised. Further, I ask who could tell me John 3:15 and there is at least an equally small number. And because you don't know verse 15 and verse 17, you will not understand verse 16. The most important word in verse 16 is "so". It does not mean that God *sooo* loved the world; it does not mean God loved the world *sooo* much. The word "so" there means "thus"; in the same way – so that's how God loved the world. The word "so" should come between the words "for" and "God" – "For so God loved the world...." And that word "so" is saying that he loved the world in the same way as he did and that refers back to verses 14 and 15. What God did in verses 14 and 15 demonstrated his love centuries before, and then: "For so God loved the world" – *in the same way*. When you read verses 14 and 15, you find that God had sent poisonous snakes that were killing off the people of Israel because they had grumbled about the food that God provided, and when they begged him to take the snakes away he said, "No, I will give you an antidote to the poison of the snakes. You have to do something. When you are bitten by a snake, go up the hill to where Moses has put a metal snake on a pole and look at that, and when you do that, you will find the poison will leave your system." Then (verse 16) he says, "For God so loved the world that he gave his only begotten Son...." In verse 15, Jesus said, "as Moses lifted up the serpent in the wilderness, even so (same word) the Son of Man must be lifted up." You see how the context is so important if you are going to understand a text? But those verse numbers mean that we look at just one text and quote it as if we know it.

I will give you just one more example of this. You must have heard the saying "a text out of context is a pretext". Well, let me give you this example. Here is a text I heard quoted recently: "I can do all things through Christ who strengthens me." Do you know that verse? I want you to think of something you can do because Christ strengthens you – anything at all that you could not do without him but you can do with him. Think of something that comes in the category of all things that you can do through Christ who strengthens you. Did you think of money? No? Well, this verse is about managing to live on the money you get. Paul is saying in that verse in Philippians that he has learned in whatever state he is, therein to be content. He is saying that if he has a lot of money coming in he is content; if he has only a little money coming in, he is content. The opposite of being content is to be covetous or greedy, and it is greedy people who can't manage their money. And isn't it amazing that the more they have, the more they want? "Godliness with contentment is great profit," said Paul. And he knew it. I am going to churches in Britain and asking them how many of them are in debt, and in the average church one third are in debt. To be in debt, according to my New Testament, is stealing. There are two ways to steal money – one is to steal money from other people and the other is to withhold money from people to whom it belongs. When you get into debt – that is, behind with payments – you are robbing people of money that belongs to them. It is serious. It is a sin in my New Testament. Now don't get me wrong – you may have a mortgaged house, you may be paying for the car bit by bit. That is not debt. Debt is when you get behind with the payment and you owe money to the other that you are not giving them, and that is stealing.

Here is a text – "I can do all things through Christ who strengthens me" – which means that I can manage on whatever money comes in or doesn't come in. And you notice that the reason he could do that was that he was content. Some of the poorest people in the world that I have met – in India for example, living on the streets – are surprisingly content. They have always challenged me because they are so content. It is a great gift to be content with whatever you have and not want what the Joneses have down the road, and not envy what others have, and not want to keep up with them, and not respond to every advertisement on TV you see, and be content and not want so much. Actually, in Britain, everybody is now living above their income, everybody, because the government is in debt as they are borrowing money every year. They actually borrow a thousand pounds for every person in Britain to keep up our standards of living. America is in the same boat and their national debt is shooting up to keep their citizens on their standard of living.

Our government said to the British people that they have to cut down, they have to pay their bills, and need to cut down the standard of living, and we have seen protests and riots as people don't want their standard of living dropped. And we are living on our grandchildren's money. They are going to have to pay it back. I think that is wicked – to be stealing from your grandchildren – but we are all doing it. And Paul says, "I can do all things through Christ who strengthens me." Whether I have a lot of money coming in or a little, I am content. What a statement! And doesn't that become a relevant text now to all of us?

So it is those text numbers which have made us into "text people" and we quote a text like that and a verse like that and think we have quoted it properly. We think we have understood it though we have ignored the verses round about it, because we can quote chapter and verse for a particular statement in the Bible. Sorry to labour that point but it is a very important point with me.

Let us go back to what I was saying: read the Bible a book at a time. Just sit down and read the whole book through before you study anything in it. Don't just study bits of a book first – study the book first and make sure you understand why that book was written and what kind of a book it is.

I have written a few books as you may know, and some of them are widely misunderstood. I wrote a book called *The Normal Christian Birth* about how to become a Christian, and the British Library, which receives a copy of every book published in Britain and categorises or classifies it for the public libraries in Britain, took my book – *The Normal Christian Birth* – and classified it under Gynaecology! So my book goes into all the public libraries under the "Medical" section. I had some very interesting letters from doctors and nurses, but it has nothing to do with gynaecology. Then my book *The Road to Hell* was advertised in a British magazine: "Read David Pawson's autobiography *The Road to Hell*" and it's nothing of the kind. When you read a book in the Bible make sure you understand what that book is. Take a simple example. There is a book in the Bible called the book of Proverbs. Strangely, it is full of proverbs – it is not a book of promises. It would be called that if it was a book of promises that God made to you, but no, it is a book of proverbs. Now a proverb is not a promise, but almost every time I have heard a preacher quote the book of Proverbs, he has been quoting it as if it is a promise that you can claim from God. A proverb is nearly always true, but not always. It is an observation of life that is usually true, but not always. Therefore you cannot claim it as a promise that always works, and if you turn the book of Proverbs into a book of promises you are going to have real problems, some disappointments. Take an example or two: There is one verse in Proverbs that says: "Train up a child in the way he should go and he will not depart therefrom." Parents have claimed that as a promise. I know many Christian parents who have claimed that as a promise. They have brought up their children in the Christian way and their children have grown up and rejected that and gone the other way, and the "promise" didn't come true. Usually it does, often it does – that if you share your gospel with your children they will stay with it. But not always. It will not always be true and there will be parents who are hurt and disappointed. It is not a promise.

The book of Proverbs also says, "In all your ways acknowledge the Lord and he will direct your paths." That is usually true but not always. It is not a promise that he will give you guidance all the way. If you try to claim that verse as a promise, you must remember that it is a proverb, and a proverb is a proverb is a proverb. It is a general observation on how life works. It is to give you wisdom, and proverbs can contradict each other.

There are two verses in the book of Proverbs that directly contradict each other, and wisdom is to know when one proverb applies in a situation or the other, because proverbs give you wisdom – general wisdom. If you read and study the book of Proverbs you will be a better person. You will be a wiser person. You will make better decisions, but don't claim them as always working for you. That would be a mistake. We have two proverbs in English, for example: "More haste, less speed", that's one; and the other is: "He who hesitates is lost". Now they contradict each other. "More haste, less speed" means don't hurry; and "He who hesitates is lost" (and we have a different version of that one – he who hesitates is ten miles from the next exit, and that's a kind of freeway proverb) is advising you not to be slow. Wisdom comes in knowing when to hurry and when to be slow, but you mustn't claim either of them to be always the right word for the right situation because you have turned it into a promise.

It was Solomon who collected the book of Proverbs and he collected them from outside Israel as well as inside. Wisdom is not confined to God's people. Ordinary proverbs contain many practical observations on life which are useful even for Christians. Solomon wrote three books in the Bible that are attributed to him – the Song of Solomon, the book of Proverbs, and the book Ecclesiastes – and if you want to get into those three books, you need to imagine what age Solomon was when he wrote them. In the Song of Solomon, he is obviously a young man deeply in love, so much filled with thoughts of his girl that he never mentions God once. And he is not the first young man to be like that, whose thoughts are all on the young girl and he forgets everybody else, even God himself. But there it is, and he wrote that when he was a young man.

Now when you come to the book of Proverbs, it is quite different. He begins, "Now my son, be careful of women. They are dangerous. Don't you be misled by bad women." How old is he? He is in his middle age. He has already sown his own wild oats. He has already made his own mistakes, now he is trying to stop his son making the same mistakes. That is what middle-aged people do. I was in one family and I heard the teenage girl say to her parents, "What did you do at my age that makes you so worried about me?" And I think that is about the most devastating question I have ever heard a teenager ask parents. But here Solomon is in the book of Proverbs: "Now son, be careful about bad women. They'll get you." He is middle-aged when writing Proverbs, and middle-aged people talk rather differently from young people.

Then you come to Ecclesiastes and he says, "Remember your Creator when you are young, before the teeth are few, before the eyes are dim, before the legs begin to shake, before you can't hear the song of the birds." How old is he now? He is an old man looking back over life, and he is trying desperately to prevent young people finishing up as disillusioned as he was, because he finished life saying that everything was pointless, it had all been a waste of time. Fancy getting to the end of your life and feeling you had wasted the only opportunity you will ever have to live it. But you see, wisdom is learning to make the right decisions, the right choices. You have only one life to live, you won't ever have today again and it is rushing by, and when you get to my age it goes so quickly. I have a theory about that: when I was twenty, one year was a twentieth of my memory; when I was forty, one year was a fortieth of my memory; when I was sixty, one year was a sixtieth; when I was eighty, one year was an eightieth – and I reckon that is why, as you age, life goes more and more quickly. Years just come and go like that. Whether my theory is right or wrong, it does that – time goes more quickly the older you get. And you can get to the end of your life just filled with regrets at the wrong choices you made, at the wasted time in your life and so, at the end of Ecclesiastes: "Remember your Creator". I can see him shaking and saying to the young people: remember your Creator in the days of your youth before the legs let you down and the eyes let you down, etc., etc. – before it all happens. You see, when he was a young man he forgot the Lord and that is why God is not mentioned in the Song of Solomon. Now he is warning young people so that they won't waste their one opportunity at life. He finishes up by saying, "Fear God and love his commandments." And I, as an old man, want to say to young people: remember your Creator. Take that from "a cute, friendly old man," as I have been described on Twitter!

We are looking at the human side of the books now and we are rebuilding the human situation out of which that book came. That helps you to understand why that book was written and why it is different from every other book. Look for the human story behind the book.

Is Everything in the Bible True?
Let me say something now that somebody is going to put on Twitter I know: There are things in the Bible that are not true. Now there is something for you to think about! Boy, will that go up in lights! Well, let us take some examples. In the book of Ecclesiastes, one of the verses says this: "I have found one man in a thousand I could respect, but not one woman." Is that true? It was true for Solomon because he had seven hundred wives and three hundred mistresses and if you have played around with women as he did, you lose all respect for women and that is the truth in that verse. It was true for him, but don't take it as God's truth for you.

Or take a bigger example: the book of Job. Most of Job is not true. It is a true record of what Job's "comforters" said – Eliphaz, Bildad and Zophar. They found Job full of self-pity, sitting on an ash heap, covered in boils, having lost his job and his children, and his wife was cursing him and saying to curse God, but he did refuse to curse God for all the disasters, and went and sat on the ash heap. The three friends came to talk to him, and the burden of their talk to Job is that he should know that he must have been a bad man to be suffering so much – a real sinner. No wonder he was suffering such loss – family, job, health. And they were wrong! At the end of the book of Job, God says they were wrong. That was not the reason he was suffering. The actual reason for his suffering was that Satan had challenged God in heaven, and Satan had said to God that people loved him because he was good to them and if he stopped blessing them they would curse him. And God had said, "Prove that." So Satan had thrown everything he had at Job to try to make Job curse God and lose his faith, and Job refused to lose his faith. He hung on to his faith even though all his friends told him to confess his sins so God would bless him again.

Actually, at the end of the book, God dealt with Job directly, and he told him a very unusual thing. Job was so depressed and God told him: "When you're depressed, meditate on the hippopotamus." I think that is lovely advice, don't you? You try it next time you are depressed and worried – just think about the hippopotamus. Well, it cured Job's depression and he came out of it. I mean, the hippopotamus is such a ridiculous animal – how could God create such a silly thing? But when you meditate like that, you cheer up, and Job did, and he said, "Lord, I'm sorry I ever doubted you. I'm sorry I grumbled. I'm sorry I've complained." Then God blessed him again with another family, with a new job and he became rich and prosperous. It is an amazing story, but every one of those comforters, those so-called friends, was giving him bad advice that was not true. They were certain that he must have sinned more than anybody else to deserve this, but it was all due to a plot in heaven, not on Earth – to the Devil saying: people only believe in you God because you bless them; take the blessings away and they will curse you. Satan was wrong. Job didn't follow Satan's design, and God was vindicated to Satan, and then because he has made Job an example of not being blessed, he blessed him more than ever at the end of the book. It is a lovely story. It is one of the oldest books in the Bible, probably written about the time of Abraham – a beautiful story. When you feel that life is unfair and God has been unjust, read the book of Job and then meditate on the hippopotamus.

Then, in the middle of the Old Testament, you get the books of Kings and the books of Chronicles, all of which cover the same history of Israel. And when you turn to the New Testament, there are four Gospels, all telling us about the life of Jesus – Matthew, Mark, Luke and John. Why four?

Repetitions have a Purpose
Well these repetitions have a purpose and I will give you a clue to the Kings and Chronicles overlap. Kings was written by a prophet and Chronicles by a priest. One was written before the exile when they were taken to Babylon, and the other was written afterwards, and that is why they are different. When the prophet wrote the history of Israel, he told them all the bad things that Israel had done which had deserved the exile, and why God had punished them, so you get David and Bathsheba there and that sordid affair, and all the bad kings of Israel. But when Chronicles describes the same history it highlights the good things in Israel because, when they came back from exile, a whole generation had died and they needed to recover three things which they were in danger of losing because of the gap.

First, they needed to recover their sense of *belonging*. They needed to be given a long family tree, a genealogy from Adam right through to their day and that is why the first few chapters of Chronicles have all the "begats" and they now knew their family roots. It is awfully good to know your roots. There is an example of a black man in America who has written a book called *Roots*. It has been made into a film and he dug back into his African roots and you find your identity when you know your roots, when you know where you have come from. It helps you to know where you are going. The first thing they needed when they came back from the exile was to know their roots. So they got six chapters of all those names which are not in the book of Kings though they cover the same period.

The next thing they needed to recover was their *royalty*. They had had a king until they went into exile and now they must rediscover the royal line of David, so Chronicles tells them where that royal line now is, so that they can look forward to having a king again.

The other thing they really needed to find again was their *religion*. So Chronicles tells us the history of the religion of Israel. It is the same period of history as Kings, but is for quite a different purpose. Now, when you read those two books, you won't ask questions as to why the two books cover the same history. They are from an entirely different point of view from each other, and that is the clue to overlap, even to the four Gospels which overlap with each other.

Why Four Gospels in the Bible?
There are things which are repeated in at least three of the Gospels and you wonder why. Why couldn't God give us one Gospel – to read the story of Jesus in one go? Some people have tried to put the four Gospels into one story. It is a very difficult task. It was tried for the first time about a thousand years ago. Then a detective novel writer in my town in England tried it. He wrote many detective stories but one book was called *The Four Gospels in One Story* and he put it together but it makes a mess because we need four Gospels to look at Jesus from four different angles – you get a fuller picture of someone when you have a different aspect of their character and their activity. Broadly speaking, Matthew presents Jesus as King of the Jews, Mark presents Jesus as Son of Man, Luke presents Jesus as Saviour of the World, and John presents Jesus as Son of God. That gives you a lovely total picture of Jesus in at least four of his functions.

But there is more to it than that. Matthew, Mark and Luke are called the synoptic Gospels because synoptic means: "syn" – together; "optic" – look. And synoptic Gospels look at Jesus from a similar view and they look at him from the outside, whereas John's Gospel looks at Jesus from the inside. That is the main reason why it is so different.

So now you can read the four Gospels in a different way but I am going to say more. Of the four Gospels, two are written for unbelievers and two for believers. Of the two for believers, one is written for young believers – new believers – and the other is written for mature believers. Do you know which? You can give the wrong Gospel to an unbeliever. Which two are written for unbelievers? Mark and Luke. Mark tells them what Jesus *did*, and Luke tells them, in addition to Mark, what Jesus *said*. Then finally John came along and talked about what Jesus *was*!

When a great person dies, interest in them goes through three phases. The first is the obituary notice which will simply list what the person did. Then people begin to be interested in what they said, and their speeches and letters are published. The third phase is when people write a book really getting in to the man and telling us from the inside, what he was. And you get this progression in the four Gospels. Mark told us what Jesus did, Matthew and Luke added in what Jesus said and then John tells us what Jesus was – the mature look that we have in the Gospel of John was written last.

Now Matthew was written for new believers and John is written for old believers. The same parable in two different Gospels carries a different message. Take the parable of the lost sheep. It occurs in Matthew and Luke, but in Luke the lost sheep is a lost unbeliever who needs to be found, while in Matthew the lost sheep is a lost believer who needs to be brought back. In Luke, the parable of the great feast is for unbelievers to be invited to come and take their place at the feast, but in Matthew the emphasis is on the man who didn't change his clothes and was thrown out of the feast at the end, "for many are called but few are chosen" at the end. So you see, even the same parable of Jesus which he obviously told on more than one occasion has a different message because of the books in which they occur which are aimed at different people.

And Matthew, of course, was not only aimed at new believers but new *Jewish* believers and has a particular approach for them. So four Gospels – all different – and you will only understand what is in each Gospel when you know who it was written for and why. Then that Gospel will have more meaning for you.

Letters in the Bible

Let us turn to another type of book in the Bible, because there are many different types of books – song books, history books, law books and letters. Now when you read a letter, you have a problem: you don't know what the situation is to which the letter is addressed. Let me illustrate that from mobile phones. Are you getting sick of people talking behind you and you turn round only to find that they are on their mobile phone? Or when you are on a bus or train and you hear someone on the phone, you are hearing only one side of the conversation and your brain tries to figure out what is happening at the other end – have you had that experience? Let us just imagine it for a moment: "Hello; has it arrived? Right. Oh! Congratulations! What does it weigh? What colour is it? Is it petrol or diesel?" You see what I mean? Your brain was trying to work out what the other person was saying and he wasn't talking about a baby, though I am sure you would have thought he was. Well now, when you get a letter that Paul had written, you don't know what was happening at the other end. You have to guess by reading the letter what was going wrong. Usually there was something going wrong – he didn't write letters unless there was. So when you read a letter you have to ask what is happening at the other end. To what situation does this correspond? For all correspondence refers to a situation. The writer talks about what is happening at the other end. Well, that is how you read a letter. You don't read it in the same way you read a history book or a law book or a song book. A song book you sing – that is the best way to read a song book. Sing a song to yourself as you read it.

Read the Bible a Book at a Time
What I have been telling you so far is that each book in the Bible is different, and you read the Bible a book at a time. That is why I've written the book *Unlocking the Bible* – to help people do just that. I would encourage people not to try to read the Bible straight through. Rather, look up the chapter of my book you are going to study and then read that book as a whole. Then start studying each little bit of it, not the other way around. Too many people read little parts first and the whole book last – or perhaps not even read the whole book ever. If you read little bits you won't ever get the message of the Bible. You may derive some personal devotional help but if you want to study the Bible it needs to be a book at a time.

Why Study the Word of God?
Now I want to speak to you about why God wants you to study his Word. Why do we do it? This is about motivation – we must have a good reason because it is going to take time. There was a businessman in New Zealand I knew and he got up an hour earlier than he used to rise, and he found he could do with an hour's less sleep. His purpose was to study the Bible for an hour every morning. He became a world famous person for God – Bill Subritzky. He would never have become known around the world as a servant of God had he not decided to get up one hour earlier to read his Bible. But then he was motivated to read it, he *wanted* to. Why did he want to? What is the point of getting to know

your Bible? Well, the Bible will not make you clever and it won't make you rich, so don't read it for either of those reasons. The Bible claims to make you wise. Do you want to be wise? Then this is the book to study. If you want to be clever, go and get another book out of the library. If you want to be rich, there are plenty of books on that. But if you want to be wise, then the Bible is the book to read. Why? Because being wise is making the right choice, making the right decision at every stage of your life so that you don't waste any of it. So read it and you won't get to the end of your life having wasted it and full of regret of what might have been.

How the Bible makes you Wise
Now, how is the Bible able to make you wise? The answer is very simple: because in this book you will find the truth and it is the truth that brings wisdom: the truth about yourself, the truth about God and the truth about the world in which we live. Once you know the truth about those three vital matters and then act upon the truth and make the right decisions, you will have a wise life and get to the end of it with few regrets. Learning the truth about yourself is not very comfortable. A dear lady said to me, "I don't read my Bible; my Bible reads me." I knew exactly what she meant. Another person said to me, "Every message in the Bible has my name and address on it." Again, I knew what they meant. When you look into the Bible, the Bible itself says you are looking into a mirror and you will see what you really are. You see, most of us have a wrong idea about ourselves. Some people have an inferiority complex – they feel they are lower than everybody else. More people have a superiority complex – they have too high a view of themselves. Too high a view or too low a view of yourself can be terribly dangerous. It is unreal, you have not accepted yourself as you really are.

But the Bible tells you the truth about yourself. It is not always comfortable, but it is profoundly helpful to know what you are really like. If you didn't think you were a sinner, just try reading your Bible and you will find out you are. But it will tell you not only what you are, it will tell you what you can be. Some people think it will just tell you what you ought to be. Well, it does that, but it only does that in order to tell you what you can be. That is lovely – to find out who you really are, what you really are, and then to find out what you ought to be, and then to find the good news: that you can be. And you realise that God has planned a life for you that he wants you to have, and it will fit you as it fits no-one else. Don't ever try to be like someone else. Be yourself in Christ. Be what he wants you to be, and that will give you a satisfying life, fitted to you. To find the truth about yourself, the truth about what you are, the truth about what you ought to be and the truth about what you can be in Christ is a lovely discovery and a vital one to making the most of your life even if it is a bit horrifying at first.

The ancient Greeks used to say the secret of wisdom was to "know yourself". But which of us can know ourselves accurately? Not too high, not too low, but just right – to get to know yourself as you really are, as you ought to be, and as you could be. Only our Bible will tell you that.

Above all, it tells you the truth about God. You know what he is really like only if you read the whole Bible. If you read only bits, you have a distorted view of God because you are just picking out the parts you like and ignoring the bits you don't like. The God of the Bible is the God who loves and hates; he is a God who heals and kills; he is a God who blesses and curses. But he doesn't do any of those things arbitrarily. There is no such thing as good luck and bad luck with God. He does it all because he is righteous and therefore he is consistent in character and you need to know God as he is, not as you would like him to be or as you think he is – but as he *really* is! And there is only one book that can give you the whole balanced truth about God.

Then it will tell you the truth about how you will relate to God and how you can relate to him and how you can become a son or daughter in his family. Only the Bible can tell you all that. That is why it says in one letter in the New Testament that, "the scriptures are able to make you wise unto salvation." It can tell you how you can be saved from yourself, and what a glory that is, what a joy that is. As you read the Old Testament and the New Testament, you get the whole picture of this God and you know what he is really like. You get to know his thoughts – how he thinks; how he thinks about you, how he thinks about the world. You get to know his feelings. Did you know that God has feelings too? Do you know, this very day, each of us has either made God happy, sad or angry? Do you know how God feels about you? That is far more important than how you feel about him because your future depends upon how he feels about you. And we affect his feelings and the Bible is full of his feelings.

God regrets things, he is disappointed, he is happy, he whistles, he sings – it is all there. When he is happy about us, he sings. There is a thought! Did you ever realise that? We are so busy singing to him, we forget that he sings about us. It is not only his feelings, but you discover his intentions, his will, and it is vital if we are going to make the most of the one life he has given us – which is over so quickly – that we find out his will for us and do it. Once you have got to know a person's thoughts and their feelings and their will, you know them! And to know God is a rich experience and the main reason why he created us: to seek him, and find him and know him – not only the truth about him, but this book will tell you the truth about this world, where it came from, why it came, why we are here, where it is going to, how history will finish. No other book can tell you that. It will tell you how it is all going to end – with a new beginning in which we can take part. Isn't that amazing? In other words, you learn to take a long view of life and not a short-term view. To take a short view of life is to concentrate on what we can do today to enjoy ourselves. To take a long view of life is to consider that what I do today is going to affect the future. It is wise to prepare for the future. It is silly not to think about it. To live for today is the heart of existentialism – to live for the now is foolish, very foolish; to live for tomorrow and the future is wise.

So the Bible tells us about our world, where it has come from and where it is going to, and it offers us a place, not only now but in the future forever. How and where we spend that future is dependent on how we use our present. Once you realise that, you take the long view. The Bible says that sin is a pleasure – for a time! It doesn't last. Nothing else is going to last. The only thing you can take into the future is your character, and that is what God is interested in, and he wants you to be wise and produce the character that you can produce in him, and which he desires for you, and which I believe, in your better moments, you long for too. So that is why you should study your Bible.

Remember too, that you, the whole of you, needs to respond to that Word, just as God is telling you his thoughts, his feelings, and his will, his intentions. He says: I don't just want you to think about the Bible, I don't just want you to feel about it (though I think *feeling* the Bible is a step forward – some people only *think* it, but when you feel it, when you are finally touching your emotions, that is a real step forward). But ultimately, it is those who *do* the Bible, who do God's will as they have discovered it in the scriptures, they are the ones who are really going to make progress. You see, it is a mirror, and if you look into the mirror and then say, "I don't like what I see", and you turn away, that has been a waste of time. So James says when you look into the Word of God and you see yourself, then be a *doer* of the Word, and not just a hearer. For it is a book of instruction that God has given us to make the very most of the life he gave us.

Thank you, Lord, for giving us that Book of instruction and telling us what we can be and what we ought to be and what, in Christ, we will be. *Amen.*

ABOUT DAVID PAWSON

A speaker and author with uncompromising faithfulness to the Holy Scriptures, David brings clarity and a message of urgency to Christians to uncover hidden treasures in God's Word.

Born in England in 1930, David began his career with a degree in Agriculture from Durham University. When God intervened and called him to become a Minister, he completed an MA in Theology at Cambridge University and served as a Chaplain in the Royal Air Force for three years. He moved on to pastor several churches, including the Millmead Centre in Guildford, which became a model for many UK church leaders. In 1979, the Lord led him into an international ministry. His current itinerant ministry is predominantly to church leaders. David and his wife Enid currently reside in the county of Hampshire in the UK.

Over the years, he has written a large number of books, booklets, and daily reading notes. His extensive and very accessible overviews of the books of the Bible have been published and recorded in *Unlocking the Bible*. Millions of copies of his teachings have been distributed in more than 120 countries, providing a solid biblical foundation.

He is reputed to be the "most influential Western preacher in China" through the broadcast of his best-selling *Unlocking the Bible* series into every Chinese province by Good TV. In the UK, David's teachings are often broadcast on Revelation TV.

Countless believers worldwide have also benefited from his generous decision in 2011 to make available his extensive audio video teaching library free of charge at www.davidpawson.org and we have recently uploaded all of David's video to a dedicated channel on www.youtube.com

TAKE A LOOK AT YOUTUBE
www.youtube.com/user/DavidPawsonMinistry

THE EXPLAINING SERIES
BIBLICAL TRUTHS SIMPLY EXPLAINED

If you have been blessed reading this book, there are more available in the series. Please register to download more booklets for free by visiting
www.explainingbiblicaltruth.global

Other booklets in the *Explaining* series will include:
The Amazing Story of Jesus
The Resurrection: *The Heart of Christianity*
Studying the Bible
Being Anointed and Filled with the Holy Spirit
New Testament Baptism
How to study a book of the Bible: Jude
The Key Steps to Becoming a Christian
What the Bible says about Money
What the Bible says about Work
Grace – *Undeserved Favour, Irresistible Force or Unconditional Forgiveness?*
Eternally secure? – *What the Bible says about being saved*
De-Greecing the Church – The impact of Greek thinking on Christian beliefs
Three texts often taken out of context:
Expounding the truth and exposing error
The Trinity
The Truth about Christmas

They will also be avaiable to purchase as print copies from:
Amazon or **www.thebookdepository.com**

UNLOCKING THE BIBLE

A unique overview of both the Old and New Testaments, from internationally acclaimed evangelical speaker and author David Pawson. *Unlocking the Bible* opens up the Word of God in a fresh and powerful way. Avoiding the small detail of verse by verse studies, it sets out the epic story of God and his people in Israel. The culture, historical background and people are introduced and the teaching applied to the modern world. Eight volumes have been brought into one compact and easy to use guide to cover both the Old and New Testaments in one massive omnibus edition. *The Old Testament: The Maker's Instructions* (The five books of law); *A Land and A Kingdom* (Joshua, Judges, Ruth, 1&2 Samuel, 1&2 Kings); *Poems of Worship and Wisdom* (Psalms, Song of Solomon, Proverbs, Ecclesiastes, Job); *Decline and Fall of an Empire* (Isaiah, Jeremiah and other prophets); *The Struggle to Survive* (Chronicles and prophets of exile); *The New Testament: The Hinge of History* (Mathew, Mark, Luke, John and Acts); *The Thirteenth Apostle* (Paul and his letters); *Through Suffering to Glory* (Hebrews, the letters of James, Peter and Jude, the Book of Revelation). Already an international bestseller.

JESUS: THE SEVEN WONDERS OF HISTORY

This book is the result of a lifetime of telling 'the greatest story ever told' around the world. David re-told it to many hundreds of young people in Kansas City, USA, who heard it with uninhibited enthusiasm, 'tweeting' on the internet about 'this cute old English gentleman' even while he was speaking.

Taking the middle section of the Apostles' Creed as a framework, David explains the fundamental facts about Jesus on which the Christian faith is based in a fresh and stimulating way. Both old and new Christians will benefit from this 'back to basics' call and find themselves falling in love with their Lord all over again.

OTHER TEACHINGS
BY DAVID PAWSON

For the most up to date list of David's Books
go to: **www.davidpawsonbooks.com**

To purchase David's Teachings
go to: **www.davidpawson.com**

Lightning Source UK Ltd.
Milton Keynes UK
UKHW021528040922
408224UK00007B/218